my Creativity JOURNAL

my Creativity JOURNAL

REDISCOVER YOUR CREATIVITY AND LIVE THE LIFE YOU TRULY WANT

Liz Dean

CICO BOOKS
LONDON NEW YORK

Published in 2018 by CICO Books
An imprint of Ryland Peters & Small Ltd
20–21 Jockey's Fields   341 E 116th St
London WC1R 4BW   New York, NY 10029

www.rylandpeters.com

10 9 8 7 6 5 4 3 2 1

Adapted from *How to Be Creative*, first published by CICO Books in 2015.

Text © Liz Dean 2015, 2018
Consultant: Professor Michael Young
Design and illustration © CICO Books 2018

A CIP catalog record for this book is available from the Library of Congress and
the British Library.

ISBN: 978-1-78249-661-8

Printed in China

Designer: Geoff Borin
Editor: Rosie Lewis
Illustrator: Amy Louise Evans

Commissioning editor: Kristine Pidkameny
Senior editor: Carmel Edmonds
Art director: Sally Powell
Head of production: Patricia Harrington
Publishing manager: Penny Craig
Publisher: Cindy Richards

Contents

introduction

We're all creative. It's what we did naturally as children, with no deadline or purpose other than pleasing ourselves–and what we can still do. Yet, as adults in a competitive marketplace, being "creative" is often perceived as a time-wasting activity that has little bearing on making a success of our lives (unless, of course, we're brilliant, famous, or both). We're told that we must put our toys or crayons aside to do "real" work. Yet recent research shows that those who value their creativity see real benefits in every other aspect of life: we can become more effective and productive in our careers and more communicative in our relationships, and, above all, reconnect with our authentic selves, so that we make life choices that support our well-being. In this book we will learn how to drop self-judgment, find the creative flow, and really please ourselves again.

Creativity is an innate part of who we are, and when we give creativity space, whether deliberately or accidentally, it manifests instantly. We all know someone who took up a new hobby because they were temporarily unable to work or otherwise be active. My close friend Karen realized that she could bake and make mosaics while she was recovering from cancer; another friend, Guy, was made redundant and discovered drawing. This is the power of creativity, to jump into the space our circumstances allow. But it needn't take enforced rest and the threat of boredom to kickstart your creativity; you can be creative at any time, and the benefits are infinite.

All you need is this book and an open mind. You might want to flick through the book and choose an exercise at random, letting your intuition guide you, or work through a whole chapter. You might scribble notes in the margins, doodle alongside the illustrations, turn down pages, or add notes of techniques you've tried. Let this journal become a record of your adventures in creativity; as it fills up, you'll find it offers you a fascinating view of yourself at the time of writing, and a valuable resource to which you can return many times over.

As you become more actively creative, you may find that the idea you begin with evolves. Your goal may initially be a memoir, but you develop an interest in making a photo collage; you may want to redesign an interior but end up writing poetry. Creativity opens up many unexpected possibilities.

I hope this book encourages you to discover and express your tastes, ideas, and talents.

BECOME AN EXPERT
ON YOURSELF, AND
KNOW WHAT LIGHTS YOUR
CREATIVE FIRE

who are you?

your personal vision

If you have creative hunger and need gentle ways to nurture yourself, you might like to begin by exploring your "personal vision." A personal vision is an expression of who you are—your likes and loves, your beliefs and goals. Many people create a focus for their immediate dreams by making vision boards, while others work with affirmations that improve the way they perceive themselves.

SAYING AFFIRMATIONS

Affirmations are short statements that you say ritually to reinforce a particular belief. They work because they program the subconscious mind to generate a positive attitude. Our thoughts create our reality—current research suggests that positive thoughts create new neural pathways in the brain, which become strengthened with habitual use—so habitually good thoughts actually affect the brain's neural networks, also helping to break negative thinking patterns.

Affirmations are also sometimes used on cards, as a way of tapping into your intuition—see page 48.

POSITIVE AFFIRMATIONS

I have everything I need to be happy and successful

Today is the day I make positive changes

I am always good enough

Everything is possible

I am guided to make the best choices for myself

I love unconditionally

I can create whatever I desire

I trust my creativity

I move forward in the knowledge that I am safe and protected

WRITE SEVEN AFFIRMATIONS FOR YOURSELF. CHOOSE ONE TO FOCUS ON AT THE START OF EACH DAY.

1

2

3

4

5

6

7

MAKE A VISION BOARD

A vision board is a collection of images that mirrors your aspirations and values.

• Think of five or six things that are important to you: perhaps family, more work or money, a piece of art or craft you'd like to make, a book you want to see published, a partner you'd like to meet, a mentor you value, a famous person you admire.

• Go through magazines and newspapers and look online to find images that represent these things, cut out or print the best ones, and create a collage here.

FIND YOUR "TRIGGER VISION"

One of the simplest ways to connect with your goals and values is the "trigger vision." A trigger vision is an everyday symbol that is meaningful to you, and instantly triggers your imagination and positive feelings.

What's your favorite animal, flower, sport, or color? Visualize it and generate positive feelings around it. Set the intention that you'll notice this trigger vision whenever it arises in your everyday life, and whenever you see it, you'll generate all its positive associations. Then let your imagination fly.

TRIGGER VISIONS

The color turquoise for the sparkling sea around the Greek island you once visited; where else might you swim in a turquoise sea?

A soccer ball and a time when your team won; what sport would you play if you knew you'd be brilliant at it?

A black cat, which makes you think of luck and home comforts; what would you love to do to make your home cozier?

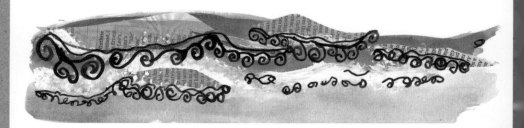

WRITE OR DRAW YOUR TRIGGER VISION.

tell your story

Through stories, we discover the truth of our human experience: just think of the many stories and movies you love because they reinforce your values or your sense of humor, or hold an important message. Many of our oldest stories–fables, fairytales, and parables–hold within them a moral message, expressed through archetypal characters and, often, magical messengers. Little Red Riding Hood should not have left the path in the woods to encounter the talking wolf; Beauty needed to love the handsome prince even when he looked like a beast. There are tales of entrapment and escape in Rapunzel, Hansel and Gretel, and Bluebeard, the jealousy of the ugly sisters in Cinderella, and the Little Match Girl's extreme poverty. Reading today's memoirs, we find the same themes: challenge, courage, transformation, and reward. In telling your own story, you write only what you, uniquely, know, while reaching out to others who have shared your experiences.

REASONS TO WRITE YOUR MEMOIR

To "write out" difficult emotions, such as guilt, anger, or loss

To share extraordinary and ordinary events that have meaning for you

To make sense of the past

To record your family history

To celebrate a family event

Because you want to

GO WITH THE FEELING

Focusing on feelings (achievement, sadness, anger, joy), rather than events, may help you to begin your story. You might also ask yourself: "What's my darkest thought/fear/belief?"

WRITE ABOUT THE PART OF YOUR LIFE THAT BRINGS UP THE MOST POWERFUL FEELINGS.

Write a little of your story every day, so that writing from your memories becomes a regular part of your present life.

YOUR FAIRY TALE

Cast yourself as a fairy-tale character, and write your story in the third person
("He/she…"). As you write more, you may feel comfortable writing in the first person,
shifting from "he/she" into "I."

ONCE UPON A TIME...

....
....
....
....
....
....
....
....
....
....
....
....
....
....
....
....
....
....

TALK TO OTHERS

Memories are stimulated by conversation. Talk to others who share or have shared part of your story, and you may find you begin to remember more.

WRITE DOWN OTHER PEOPLE'S MEMORIES OF YOU.

Keep a notebook with you and jot down ideas for your life story as they come, or record them on your phone. You might begin a scrapbook for memorabilia, or draw what you recall.

KEEP A DIARY

You may or may not have old diaries to lead you back into memories of your earlier years, but regardless, beginning a diary now will help you foster a regular habit of writing and creativity–as well as giving you material for the future. There's also an intimacy that comes with writing a diary, and the perception that we reveal our secrets to a diary as though to a mute friend. Treat your diary like a confessor to get comfortable with disclosing parts of yourself to the page.

WRITE SOME OF YOUR SECRETS.

"The diary taught me that it is in the moments of emotional crisis that human beings reveal themselves most accurately. I learned to choose the heightened moments because they are the moments of revelation."

Anaïs Nin, in her essay "On Writing"

CREATE A COLLECTION

Collect material for your story by tracking down old school exercise books, photographs, greetings cards, and diaries. Make a space in your home to gather everything that's connected with your research. Add objects that have sentimental value: a cracked bowl that you mended because it's too precious to discard; a piece of jewelry given to you by a close friend whom you don't see any more; some stones from a beach where you spent a vacation; a leaving card from your old workplace (whatever happened to that guy in accounts you spent four years in meetings with?). Each object has its own story to tell.

Make a piece of art from your memories. Arrange your memory items into themes or a timeline. Display them together, or take photographs of the items and create a montage to frame.

CHOOSE ONE OF YOUR MEMORY ITEMS. WHY HAVE YOU CHOSEN IT? WHEN IN YOUR LIFE IS IT FROM? WHAT'S THE STORY BEHIND IT?

do what you're good at

Your interests, and doing what you love, are the material for any project you'd like to evolve. For some of you, it may be clear already what you love doing. Music may be your thing, or craft, sport, family history: this is all material for your creative work. Yet some skills are more subtle, and because of this some people say: "I'm not creative or talented," or "I'm a good all-rounder—I don't know if there is one thing I can do." Everyone has one or more talents or skills.

TALENTS YOU MAY HAVE

Being a good host

Caring for others

Solving problems

Understanding animals

Making your home a sacred place

Fixing cars

Being the family networker

Never getting lost

Being able to sail a boat or drive a car

MAKE A LIST OF YOUR TALENTS. (IF YOU'RE NOT SURE WHAT YOU'RE GOOD AT, ASK A FRIEND OR FAMILY MEMBER TO HELP YOU.)

- ....
- ....
- ....
- ....
- ....
- ....
- ....
- ....
- ....
- ....
- ....
- ....
- ....
- ....
- ....
- ....

WAYS TO USE YOUR TALENTS

Here are just a few ways of applying your skills creatively:

• If you're an organizer, apply this to your home—you might be a great organizer at work, but now get decluttering and put your house in order, or devise a color scheme for your walls.

• If you're a great host, the next time you bring people together, think of creative ways your guests can connect (a foodie theme, inviting people whose names begin with A …).

• If family history captivates you, make a storyboard of photographs or scanned images into a card for a relative, or turn it into a piece of framed art for your home or to give as a gift. Write a poem about the life you imagine one of your ancestors had. Find a way to visit an area where your relatives once lived; take photographs. Embroider a family tree.

YOUR TALENTS ARE YOUR MATERIAL

WRITE 5 WAYS YOU COULD USE YOUR TALENTS FOR A CREATIVE PROJECT.

1

2

3

4

5

CONSIDER YOUR ACHIEVEMENTS

When a tricky problem arises, it can feel as if we've never encountered it before. Yet we have successfully dealt with thousands of challenges in our lives, from learning to cross the road through passing a driving test, and from putting words on a blank page through dividing a restaurant check among 14 people. At an emotional level, we have learned many lessons: we may have successfully managed loneliness, confronted an aggressive colleague, learned to give without expecting reward.

Think back and identify what you consider to be your greatest tests and achievements, those that give you the strongest feelings. You might find that you remember occasions that got buried. You might begin with your obvious successes, then unearth something deeper, more rewarding. Then consider how it felt when you achieved your goal. Generate that feeling of breakthrough, and give it a name.

Use these words as triggers when you need reminding of your past success; this will help you feel confident about your ability to solve a present dilemma. Imagine you have a fishing rod, and you're fishing out your feel-good phrase. Allow the phrase to connect with the positive feeling you experience.

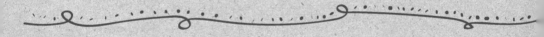

TRIGGER WORDS AND PHRASES

Quitting a bad habit: "fresh air" for smoking,
"confident me" for losing weight

Successful creative projects: "gold star," "fulfillment"

A life-changing conversation: "words with XX"
or "words about XX [event]"

Recovery from illness: "freedom," "pain-free," "happy-healthy"

WRITE DOWN FIVE OF YOUR ACHIEVEMENTS, WITH A TRIGGER WORD OR PHRASE FOR EACH ONE.

1. TRIGGER WORD OR PHRASE:

....

....

....

2. TRIGGER WORD OR PHRASE:

....

....

....

3. TRIGGER WORD OR PHRASE:

....

....

....

4. TRIGGER WORD OR PHRASE:

....

....

....

5. TRIGGER WORD OR PHRASE:

....

....

....

WHEN YOU'RE DOING WHAT YOU LOVE, YOU'RE ENTERING A STATE OF CREATIVE FLOW

do what you love

All too often, we get hooked on the outcome of a project rather than the process of creating it–that is, being in the flow (see below). While it's almost irresistible to dream of success and acknowledgment, this means staking a project on other people's approval, rather than creating for the sake of it. This bypasses the learning experience a project can offer us personally, and ties up its potential success with things or people outside our control. Success should be measured by our enjoyment of our personal creativity and playfulness.

Many entrepreneurs encounter negativity and even ridicule when they first begin. If they allowed these reactions to affect them, they might even stop their creative work altogether–but a common trait in many of these individuals is that they decide that, even if no one likes what they do, they'll do it anyway, simply because they enjoy it. They put their need to be creative above other people's opinions. I'm not saying that anyone should ignore constructive feedback, but do keep the focus on entertaining yourself. That way, your work will hold your passion.

HOW TO KNOW WHEN YOU'RE IN THE FLOW

You feel immersed and engaged

The work feels spontaneous

You can't not do what you're doing

You're unaware, or less aware, of time

You feel happy/excited/content/complete

You feel motivated to make a meaningful contribution

GET INTO A PLAYFUL MINDSET

Ben & Jerry's ice cream stems from childhood friends Ben Cohen and Jerry Greenfield, who worked as students in an ice-cream van, learned to make ice cream on a farm, and liked it. Cohen couldn't taste much and he doesn't have a sense of smell, so when they decided to make their own ice cream, he made up flavors he could taste–just for him.

Make up some ice-cream flavors. Put as many tastes together as you like (hedgehog and brandy?), then go more esoteric–seashore and honey; you get the picture. Now visualize how certain colors, objects, or even experiences might taste: a wedding, disappointment, white linen. Keep inventing.

DESCRIBE YOUR ICE CREAM FLAVORS.

WHAT WOULD YOU DO TODAY IF YOU HAD ONLY TO PLEASE YOURSELF?

creativity and positivity

It's easier to be creative when you feel positive. Research shows that those who suffer from anxiety and depression tend to find it more difficult to be creative than those with a more positive outlook. The irony is that being creative can help to generate happiness– but if you're anxious you may find it more difficult to get started. The following pages will help you to think more positively.

WRITE ABOUT A HAPPY MEMORY.

NAME THREE THINGS YOU'RE THANKFUL FOR—AND WHY.

WRITE ABOUT A PERSON AND/OR A PET YOU ADORE.

BE YOUR BIGGEST FAN

Self-compassion isn't selfish. As self-compassion researcher Dr. Kristin Neff says, "the biggest reason people aren't more self-compassionate is that they are afraid they'll become more self-indulgent. They believe that self-criticism is what keeps them in line."

We're programmed to be "good" and put others first, but genuine kindness begins with self-compassion. When we understand our own needs and do our best to meet them, we can be compassionate to others appropriately, and without resentment. For today, do not criticize yourself. Accept all your feelings and treat them equally. As the thirteenth-century Persian poet and mystic Rumi said, "This being human is a guest house": we should invite in each morning's arrivals—our emotions—with joy.

BE your
OWN best
FRIEND

WRITE SOME WORDS OF COMPASSION FOR YOURSELF THAT YOU CAN
READ AGAIN WHEN YOU'RE SAD OR UNHAPPY.

REWARD YOURSELF

It's important to recognize reasons to reward yourself without the excuse of a special occasion, whether it's for your achievements (any size), for your best characteristics (being kind, hard-working, funny …), or even simply because it's Tuesday!

REWARDS YOU MIGHT LIKE

Try yoga karaoke (singing loudly to your favorite anthems as you do the Downward Dog)

Go to a movie on your own

Take a two-hour bath

Invent ridiculous reasons to celebrate: bake a banana cake because it's Tuesday and it's raining

Hold a party in honor of a shelf you've managed to put up single-handed

LIST 5 REASONS TO REWARD YOURSELF.

1

2

3

4

5

RELAX FOR CREATIVITY

A relaxed state of mind supports creativity. When we're relaxed, our thoughts are positive, we feel happier, and ideas flow. Choose one or more activity each day for yourself, just for relaxation.

WAYS TO RELAX

Listening to, playing, or moving to music

Movement: yoga, stretching, dancing

Baking

Rearranging a display

Gardening

Walking

Tidying

Doing something that makes you laugh

wear another hat

Sometimes it can be liberating to wear a different hat—that is, try being someone that's not who you usually are, or doing something that's not what you usually do. In doing so, we may learn more about ourselves and tap into the dreams we haven't admitted to ourselves, which can provide a way into a creative life.

STEP INTO YOUR ALTER EGO

Your alter ego is the most compelling version of yourself that you can imagine. He or she may be villainous, glamorous, geeky, athletic, pedantic, or brave. How would this version of you respond to the email you've just read, the problem you're about to tackle, an event you're organizing? Your alter ego may just offer you an ingenious approach or idea.

Many movie and story plots depend on the tension between double identities, Clark Kent and Superman, Don Diego de la Vega and Zorro, or the secret heroism of "everyday" people: Eva, a grandmother in William Boyd's award-winning novel *Restless* (2006), had a secret past as a World War II spy, and feared exposure and reprisals. Authors themselves may opt for a different pen name when writing in a new genre, to liberate them from the pressure to succeed; for example, J. K. Rowling wrote her first crime novel, *The Cuckoo's Calling*, as Robert Galbraith.

MY ALTER-EGO IS CALLED.....

....

DRAW OR DESCRIBE YOUR ALTER-EGO.

INSIDE OUT

Are you an extrovert or an introvert? Here's a quick test: do you recharge by being alone (introvert), or feel energized by being with other people (extrovert)? Spending one day practicing the behavior of your "opposite" mode gets you out of your comfort zone, helping you to see a problem with a fresh perspective.

• If you're naturally an introvert, try behaving like an extrovert for one day. Plan a day that will take you into maximum contact with people: store up phone calls to return; shop with the intention to communicate with assistants; use public transport.

• If you're naturally an extrovert, try behaving like an introvert for one day. Avoid talking to people. Stick to essential emails and texts only, and do this first thing in the morning. Then switch off your phone; avoid the compulsion to communicate. This is time just for you, to make space for your own ideas. Stay home, or walk alone. Read; think; look out of the window.

AT THE END OF THE DAY, WRITE ABOUT YOUR EXPERIENCE AS AN INTROVERT OR EXTROVERT. WHAT NEW INSIGHTS DO YOU HAVE?

become intuitive

Intuition is our inner knowing, an innate wisdom that may run contrary to accepted logic and rational thought. Acting on intuition not only benefits our creative projects, but all life areas. It keeps us on the right path, protects us from potential hurt, or senses opportunity and propels us toward it. Intuition tells us when to say yes and when to say no. And if we don't heed those messages first time around, intuition is forgiving. It returns, again and again, nudging us until we listen.

No matter how intuitive you believe you are, intuition can be developed. By connecting more with your senses—the receptors of intuition—you can allow your intuition to be felt. It might manifest as excitement and a feeling of anticipation when you're in creative flow; an inexplicably good feeling about a person you've just met; or anxiety or a dull, unsettled sensation in the pit of the stomach when a situation just doesn't feel right (although your logical left brain is telling you that everything should be okay). Alternatively, you might hear an intuitive voice giving an instruction.

WHEN WE
FOLLOW OUR
INTUITION,
WE TRUST THE
TRUTHS WE SENSE
WITHIN

THE CREATIVITY CONNECTION

Intuition and creativity function in the right brain, the zone of emotions, dreams, the unconscious, and symbols. An intuitive feeling and a creative impulse often occur in similar circumstances, and share similar attributes.

HOW INTUITION MANIFESTS

Intuition strikes when we don't expect it;
it's often instant.

It doesn't always fit with your plans or expectations.

Intuition is felt through your senses.

You may get intuitive messages in a dream.

Intuition likes quiet moments, when the left brain is not busy: times of reflection, meditation, or prayer.

The ability to follow intuition may be blocked by fear, doubt, or low self-esteem.

An intuitive message (a feeling, a knowing) keeps coming back if at first you don't follow it.

When you follow your intuition and take action, there's a sense of relief and/or reward.

The more you follow your inner knowing, the more content you feel; life becomes better.

WRITE ABOUT A TIME WHEN YOU'VE SENSED YOUR INTUITION.

WORKING WITH AFFIRMATION CARDS

Affirmation cards help you connect with your intuition by offering insight and inspiration in the form of words and images. The cards act as a springboard for what is unseen. Simply shuffle the cards, and ask a question, such as "What will inspire me today?" Take one card from the top of the deck, turn it face up, and interpret it according to the words, image, number, or color on the card. Use your feelings to intuit the meaning that is right for you.

You could create your own cards by writing out a set of 11 cards or pieces of paper with one number on each. The meanings can be as below, or you can invent your own.

AFFIRMATION CARD MEANINGS

1 New beginnings, ideas

2 Love, friendship

3 Creativity, productivity

4 Stability, planning

5 Negotiation, challenges

6 Harmony, peace, balance

7 Endurance, work

8 Travel, change

9 Self-expression, determination

10 Finding completion

11 Trusting your intuition

DESIGN ONE OF YOUR AFFIRMATION CARDS.

WHAT TEXT WILL IT HAVE?

WHAT COLORS OR IMAGES?

You could also work with
one of the many affirmation
or oracle decks already
available (see page 144).

BEING IN THE MOMENT
ALLOWS SPACE
FOR YOUR CREATIVITY
TO FLOW

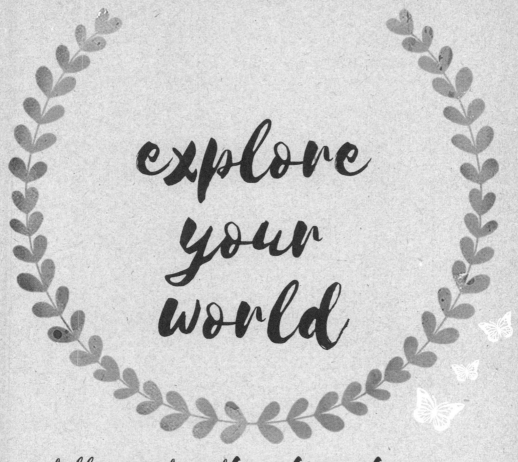

explore your world

tell your story through your home

How many times have you heard the phrase "If walls could talk"? Walls–and all the spaces we inhabit–are witnesses of our emotions and experiences. One simple way to begin to express your creativity is to cast your eye over the surfaces of your home.

"Who looks outside, dreams; who looks inside, awakes."

Carl Jung

DOES YOUR HOME REFLECT YOU?

Take a look at your home. Walk into each room with a fresh eye, as if you were a realtor or a new friend visiting for the first time. Does your home reflect your personal taste, interests, and beliefs? Perhaps your rooms are crowded with items that reflect the people you live with–such as children, a partner, or friends. Maybe the décor is bland because the builder or landlord chose it. But even if your personal space is limited or redecorating comes with a level of restriction, there's always a way for your personality to shine: in the objects you display and the pictures you hang on the walls.

WHAT DOES YOUR HOME SAY ABOUT YOU?

If you and your home feel out of sync, read through the "Block" attitudes questions on pages 102–103.

53

IMAGINE YOUR DREAM HOUSE. DRAW IT HERE. YOU MIGHT WANT TO CREATE A FLOORPLAN, OR FOCUS ON ONE ROOM. LET YOUR IMAGINATION FLOW.

awaken the senses

Tuning into our senses and the rich territory of the unconscious mind can strengthen our intuition. Connecting to our senses through the body helps us step out of thinking mode into feeling mode, tapping into our unconscious knowing. When we become more present to our senses through our body, we open up a communication pathway to our intuition. One way to do this is to connect with nature.

CONNECT WITH NATURE

Walk outdoors or sit in your yard or on your terrace or balcony if this is a peaceful space for you, and if it has plants and/or trees. Rather than purely observing what's around you, choose something to touch: the bark of a tree, a leaf, a cold park railing. You might pick up a scent (mown grass, candy, damp dog). Touching and scenting in this way will ground you in the here and now. Being present to your environment heightens your senses. Notice the people around you. Are they really here, too—or on their phones, distracted?

WHAT DID YOU NOTICE WHEN CONSCIOUSLY CONNECTING WITH NATURE?

BE AN ACTIVE LISTENER

Today, be an "active" listener, ready to engage fully with everyone you encounter. Often, we don't listen enough: we begin a conversation with an agenda, hear the other person speaking, and, rather than being open to what they have to say, rehearse what we're going to say when they've finished.

When we listen actively, we step into a powerful place—the present moment, in which anything is possible. We're able to read the nuances in their language, really understand what they are trying to communicate, and respond appropriately. I'm sure you've met active listeners before—those people who make you feel you're the most important person to them, even for the one minute you share.

They nod, gesture, and give you space to complete your sentences. They may repeat part of your conversation to ensure they've fully understood you. You feel they appreciate everything you have said, and that it's important. You feel good afterward.

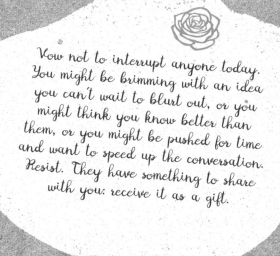

Vow not to interrupt anyone today. You might be brimming with an idea you can't wait to blurt out, or you might think you know better than them, or you might be pushed for time and want to speed up the conversation. Resist. They have something to share with you: receive it as a gift.

SLOW DOWN

AND

LISTEN

MAKE A SOUND DIARY

Creating a sound diary can make you aware of just how many different noises there are in any one place at any one time, and can also provide inspiration for creative projects.

• Download a recording app onto your phone or use Voice Memo.

• Go to a shopping mall, out for a stroll, or to an arts or sporting event, or use public transport, and record what you hear. You might record your feet crunching through snow, two people talking about a movie they watched, or someone asking for directions. You can even record snippets of conversation or activities in your home.

• Play back your sound diary a day or two later. See how you naturally connect some of the sounds. Maybe words begin to sound rhythmic, or the sound of pots and flatware (cutlery) chiming in your kitchen begins to take on the form of a conversation. You might use this as your starting point for a piece of sound art, a story, or a poem.

LIST ANY IDEAS YOU'VE HAD FROM YOUR SOUND DIARY.

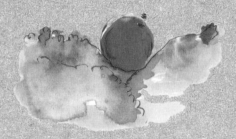

OTHER WAYS TO AWAKEN THE SENSES

• Find quiet time. This might be on your walk, or a few moments at home when you can sit in stillness. Close your eyes and focus just on the sound of your breath and the movement in your body: your shoulders rising and falling, the feeling of your lungs filling with air and then letting go. Visualize your mind emptying, as though water is flowing out of a pitcher. Keep the focus on your senses, and become aware of every sensation you feel. Let sensation fill you up. You might sense a color, a feeling, a knowing.

• Listen to music. Choose a track that reminds you of a joyful occasion. This time, when you listen, focus on one aspect of the music–perhaps the bassline, melody, or accompaniment–tuning in to each note and its rhythm. See if you can notice something in the music you haven't heard before. If you can play a musical instrument–piano, recorder, harmonica, whatever–play it, or just drum out a rhythm on your desk.

• Hold an object that is meaningful to you for a minute or two–a piece of jewelry or other keepsake, or a stone you brought home from the park or beach that connects you with the positive experience you had in that place. You might like to hold a crystal such as labradorite or amethyst, for intuition, or turquoise, for communication. Feel the surfaces of your object and begin to sense its subtle vibration in your palm.

CHANGE YOUR ENVIRONMENT

If you work during the day, vow to leave your desk for 20 minutes at lunchtime and walk around the outside of the office, go to the park, go see a building close by, or browse in a store; changing your environment can help you to get the most out of the time you have, particularly if you treat yourself to a brief visit to a new place. New experiences help us to cultivate an attitude of openness, which feeds creativity.

LOOK AROUND YOU

On your first trip out of the home this morning, look around you. A mailbox hanging open, a huge cloud, a postal worker rushing to your neighbor's door with a parcel, flowers flattened by a rainstorm, one stiletto abandoned atop a trashcan? Maybe take a photo. Does the photo tell a story?

WHAT AROUND YOU APPEARS DIFFERENT FROM YESTERDAY?

Post your photo on social media in the spirit of curiosity: there's a wealth of difference between "Here's the lasagna I ate last night" and "Wonder what happened to that stiletto-wearer ..."

FIND THE BEAUTY

Artists excel in making extraordinary artworks from ordinary objects–from cigarette sculptures through mosaics made from M&Ms. Arranging such mundane items en masse can give them new significance.

- Start your own collection: every day, collect little pieces of the ordinary to make extraordinary: receipts from a store; public transport or dry-cleaning tickets; ring pulls from soda cans.

- Create a new context for them, such as the opposite of their original purpose.

COLLECTIONS AND POSSIBLE OPPOSITE THEMES

Train or bus tickets: road/air transport theme
(papier mâché birds ...).

Dry-cleaning receipts: water themes
(boats, swimming, fish ...).

Junk mail: personal/impersonal themes
(a collage of your family's names ...).

Plastic knives, forks, and spoons: fast food or fine-dining theme
(a chandelier mobile from plastic teaspoons ...).

Try creating a physical sculpture or a video of you making your art, or arrange it on a flat surface and take a photograph.

LET GO

The act of destruction in art is often seen as an act of liberation. In letting go of material possessions, we release our attachment to them—and create a whole new perspective.

British artist Michael Landy's performance piece "Break Down" (2001) consisted of a conveyor belt, a shredder, ten workers, and all his possessions—including his artworks.

Landy catalogued everything—7,227 items in all—then hired an empty store on Oxford Street, London's principal shopping street, and with his workers destroyed everything he owned, including his clothes and food, over two weeks. He received no payment for the work, and when it was over, he had nothing apart from the clothes he was wearing and his car. The work has been seen as a statement about consumption and consumerism. Landy explains, "I had my own place to live, I had some furniture, I had some money in my bank account, then I stopped and thought about how I'm going to screw all this up … and what does this all mean, now that I can buy suits for £1,000? … and then it just came to me that I wanted to destroy all my personal belongings." Rather than feeling loss and regret, Landy experienced his installation, which attracted around 45,000 visitors, as "a really joyous occasion."

What you could make that is temporary, and what could you destroy or abandon?'

mindful ways to creativity

Mindfulness techniques are a great way to find peace, reconnect with ourselves, and make space for our creativity to thrive. May people who practice mindfulness find that it can create a sense of time slowing down, because it invites us to focus on the moment, the here and now, and experience ourselves wherever we are, slowly and without judgment.

SLOW DOWN AND APPRECIATE EACH MOMENT AS IT ARRIVES

TAKE A NEW ROUTE TO WORK

Think about the first time you drove or walked to a new place of work. You probably absorbed everything around you—the sound of the traffic, a tree just in leaf on the left-hand side of the road, the kind of people walking nearby (office workers, children going to school, a strange guy with a clipboard …). It may have felt like a long way. Yet after weeks, months, or years of doing the same route, we can arrive at work barely remembering how we got there. Each morning, the journey has passed by in a flash, as if time speeds up whenever we make that same trip.

When we slow down and go about mindfully, we really notice what's happening, and in this noticing our senses become sharper and our imagination comes in to play.

Try going to work a different way from usual and see what you discover.

WHAT DID YOU SEE ON YOUR NEW ROUTE TO WORK?
HOW DID IT MAKE YOU FEEL?

CONTEMPLATE AN OBJECT

When we look at things mindfully, something old and familiar can seem brand new; we experience it with fresh awareness, curiosity, and even wonder.

Choose an object in your eyeline. Contemplate it. Describe it. What color is it? Is it really only one color, or is it in fact made up of several shades? Is it smooth or hard? Shiny or dull?

DESCRIBE YOUR CHOSEN OBJECT.

MINDFUL EATING

Eat mindfully, without the computer or television in front of you. Before you eat, look at the colors on your plate. Take a small bite, and feel its texture on your tongue. Chew slowly and savor every mouthful. You may find yourself thinking about where the food on your plate has come from. You might begin to feel grateful to the earth for giving you your food. Maybe you recall a feeling triggered by a taste. Is it sour or sweet? What other things in life have felt this sweet?

WRITE ABOUT YOUR MINDFUL EATING EXPERIENCE.

THE MINDFUL WALK

Walking is something we do every day, often without awareness. Walking with
the intention of being mindful of your thoughts, sensations, and the environment
can help you to feel calmer and reconnect with your creative self as you pay attention
to where you are.

- Decide where you'd like to walk. Set the intention that your walking will be mindful,
and leave your cell phone at home.

- Begin to walk by really sensing your feet on the ground as you plant them with each
step. Generate the feeling that you are connecting with the earth. How does this feel?
Become aware of your body's movement–your arms swinging gently, the position of
your head. What can you see and sense?

- Focus on your breathing. In meditation practice, becoming aware of your breathing is
a technique that is used to help you be in the moment. If you feel distracted at any point
or begin to overthink, simply invite yourself to return to the breath.

WHAT DID YOU EXPERIENCE ON YOUR MINDFUL WALK?

WHEN YOU VALUE
YOUR TIME,
YOUR WHOLE LIFE
APPROACH
BEGINS TO SHIFT

starting your creative journey

set a daily intention

Setting an intention is like making a wish or saying a prayer. Each morning you can set an intention for the day ahead, asking that your day turns out a certain way.

• Speak your intention or write it down. Say, simply, what you would like to happen today (avoid saying what you don't want, as this gives energy to a negative statement). Your decision that your day should be a good, creative experience is powerful enough on its own—you don't need to be desperate, or have a grand goal in mind.

• Now feel your wish as if it has been granted. Generate a sense of joy, relief, relaxation—however you want to feel—and imagine it strongly. Add the timescale for your wish to be delivered, then consciously let go of the wish, with complete trust that you will get what you need. Place your manifesting "order" only once.

• Go ahead with the rest of your day, but pay close attention to your senses, along with conversations and communications (emails, phone calls, and texts), to make sure that you notice your gift arriving.

ALIGN YOUR
POSITIVE ENERGY
WITH UNIVERSAL ENERGY
TO CREATE SOMETHING
TOGETHER

be playful

Play is the state of mind triggered by an activity, rather than the activity itself. When we play, happy emotions are triggered. We want to play again to experience those joyful emotions. (Remember when you played a game as a child and instantly wanted to play it again … and again?) Play therefore has emotional benefits for us; we're instinctively meant to play, so allow yourself the space to have fun, rather than stepping in to judge your activity.

When we are absorbed in our activity, without the pressure of goals, comparison, or competition, we receive the reward of happy feelings. And creativity is easier when we're happy, which is why accessing a state of playfulness can be our springboard into creativity.

HOW WE KNOW WE'RE PLAYING

Being fully engaged and in the "flow"

Having no sense of time

Not being self-conscious or feeling observed

Feeling happy, even laughing

Feeling rewarded

Feeling that your body knows what it wants to do

Feeling energized

Enjoying it regardless of the outcome

Wanting to do it again

WAYS THAT PLAY SPARKS CREATIVE IDEAS

• Retrieving photos on your computer and playing with the scale because it's entertaining to elongate your nose or to see your cat bright blue might offer an unexpected idea.

• Making fondant flowers might begin as a half-hour task and go on for hours when you discover that you like doing it, and begin trying different shapes and colors.

• Dancing or playing music might take you to a different place within yourself, when you're completely captivated by rhythm, as if another part of you comes out to play.

WRITE DOWN 3 WAYS THAT YOU COULD PLAY ...

1

2

3

...NOW GO AHEAD AND DO THEM!

THE REBEL DOODLE

The appeal of the doodle is that it's fun. Commonly, we doodle when we're not supposed to—during business meetings, while on long phone calls—and of course we all doodled in the margins of our school books during lessons.

Doodling is an expression of the unconscious mind that happens when our focus should be on another task; it's as if the creative part of us wants to have fun, to rebel, while we're supposed to be at our most adult and serious (which is why we may doodle more in formal, organized meetings).

HAVE A DOODLE——ESPECIALLY IF YOU'RE SUPPOSED TO BE DOING SOMETHING ELSE RIGHT NOW!

REVIEW YOUR DOODLES

Take a look at your doodles after a few days. What did you doodle? Common motifs are flowers, arrows, cubes, faces, patterns, and landscapes, but you may have doodled something else.

Your doodles may provide an insight into a way you might approach a piece of work. For example, faces may suggest that there are people you need to collaborate with (see page 138); arrows might point to a clear sense of direction, a need to emphasize an aspect of your work or, literally, an idea for an illustration project. While these interpretations may or may not hit the mark with you, the purpose of the exercise is to explore the meanings of your own doodles and appreciate that all your output, even a doodle, has creative potential.

WHAT ARE THE CLUES IN YOUR DOODLES?

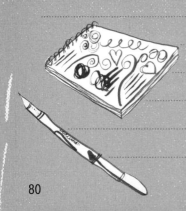

the art of boredom

As children, we probably knew boredom quite well. Dragged around shopping malls or filling long summer vacations, we grew up accepting that boredom was part of living– the bit that made the better parts, such as birthday parties, more exciting by contrast. Yet as adults, cultural pressures have made us averse even to admitting that we're a bit bored; in fact, to do so might imply that we are boring.

Yet creativity depends on mild, intermittent boredom. Boredom allows you to be yourself in a more relaxed, quietly creative mode. Reducing stimulus to our brain allows us to recharge. If we decide to allow ourselves to become a little bit bored, we make room for creative regeneration. We begin to self-entertain–to play, maybe bake, rearrange, daydream, remember an event long forgotten, or muse on what we'd like to be doing. Our observations, along with our rich internal store of memories, experiences, and ideas, are our creative resources, which feed our imagination.

"If something is boring after two minutes, try it for four minutes. If still boring, then eight. Then sixteen. Then thirty-two. Eventually one discovers that it is not boring after all."

John Cage, composer

ENJOYING

"NON-DOING," WHEN YOU CAN SIMPLY "BE," FEEDS THE CREATIVE SOUL

EMBRACING BOREDOM

You can usually choose to stay mildly bored or to distract yourself; but always choosing to tune out with computer games, emailing, eating, channel-hopping, or seeking external excitement and stimulation avoids the uncertainty of boredom—and creativity needs uncertainty to thrive. With uncertainty comes the possibility of change.

In the West, we're programmed by advertising and the movie industry to need and expect drama and the promise of entertainment. We're geared to resist boredom. Don't resist; prepare to be bored. Engage with it, and tune in to how it feels.

• Give the word "boredom" a qualifier to make it feel creatively positive, such as "good boredom" or "open time."

• Make space in your diary for unstructured personal time, with no allocated tasks. You might feel uncomfortable or even anxious about this concept because you're inviting the possibility of boredom.

• Avoid over-planning. It's tempting to do this when a free weekend yawns ahead, and fill it with back-to-back distractions. But how many times have you liked the thought of busy-ness rather than the reality?

• Daydream. Look at the clouds for a bit and see what you can make out. There may be shapes you like, or that seem to mean something to you.

make creativity a priority

Many people claim that they don't have time to be creative. But creativity is a necessity, not a luxury or an indulgence; it is essential for our well-being. We build exercise into our schedules because it's important for good health, but if we don't make real time for creativity, we're denying ourselves the expression of a fundamental aspect of what it means to be human.

Creative projects give us energy, while tune-outs (channel-hopping, checking our phones, browsing the net, or snacking) deplete it. If you make a list of activities that give you a buzz, you'll find it's the activities that nurture your creativity, rather than tune-outs, which leave you feeling flat and guilty. And good pursuits don't have to be what we'd traditionally define as "artistic"; whatever you love doing is creative work.

WE ALL HAVE A NATURAL NEED TO CREATE

WHAT ARE YOUR TUNE-OUT ACTIVITIES?

○ ....

○ ....

○ ....

○ ....

○ ....

○ ....

○ ....

WHAT ACTIVITIES GIVE YOU A BUZZ?

○ ....

○ ....

○ ....

○ ....

○ ....

○ ....

○ ....

WAYS TO MAKE TIME FOR CREATIVITY

• Make a commitment to your creativity by scheduling a weekly date to create. Put your creative slot in your phone calendar or diary at the beginning of each week.

• Protect your creative time. Other than for emergencies, make this time sacred. Choose your creativity over other daily demands: meeting with friends, or doing the laundry.

• Write down your mental clutter–scribble a list of what's on your mind, trust that you'll deal with it when you have to (and not now), then put it aside. This helps you to focus on the present to get the most out of the creative slot you've allocated for yourself. (One of your creative slots might be mindfulness practice, which can give the sensation of time actually expanding–see the mindfulness practices on pages 66-71.)

• If you find it difficult to shift from work/overthinking mode, try the creative crunch practice (see page 109).

A LITTLE DAILY RITUAL

Get into the mindset of making time for your creativity by waking up ten minutes earlier each day for six days–that's one hour in total. Spend that time making a list of ideas, or setting a general intention for how you'd like your day to turn out: setting a goal, or just being calm, or having courage if there's a challenge you'll need to deal with, for example.

If you're a morning person, getting up early to spend time on your project might work for you–the poet Sylvia Plath would get up before dawn to write while her young children were still asleep.

MAKE YOUR MORNING LISTS HERE.

DAY 1

....
....
....
....
....

DAY 2

....
....
....
....
....

DAY 3

....
....
....
....
....

DAY 4

....
....
....
....
....

DAY 5

....
....
....
....
....

DAY 6

....
....
....
....
....

MAKE AN INFOGRAPHIC

Examining how you spend your time can make it easier to schedule in time for yourself and creativity. You can do this by filling in two blank clock dials (one for AM and one for PM) at the end of each day, estimating how much time you've spent on different areas of your life. Use a different color for each type of activity. For example, green for sleep, pink for exercise. It might look something like this:

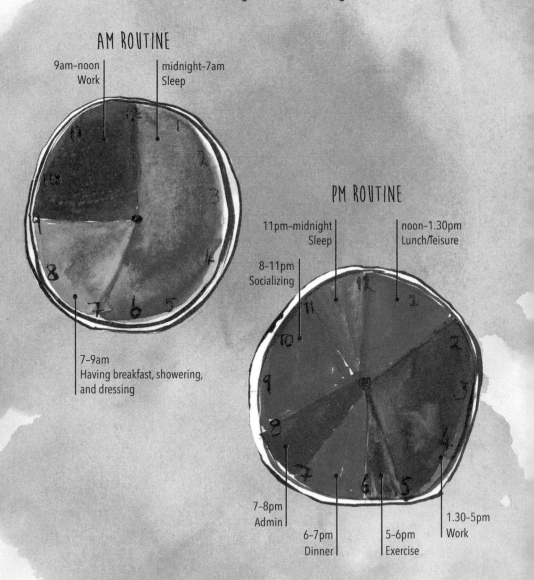

AM ROUTINE

9am–noon
Work

midnight–7am
Sleep

7–9am
Having breakfast, showering, and dressing

PM ROUTINE

11pm–midnight
Sleep

8–11pm
Socializing

noon–1.30pm
Lunch/leisure

7–8pm
Admin

6–7pm
Dinner

5–6pm
Exercise

1.30–5pm
Work

FOR THE NEXT THREE DAYS, FILL IN THE DIALS AT THE END OF THE DAY,
LOGGING HOW MUCH TIME YOU'VE SPENT ON DIFFERENT AREAS OF YOUR LIFE.

DAY 1

AM ROUTINE

PM ROUTINE

AM ROUTINE

PM ROUTINE

AM ROUTINE

PM ROUTINE

FOR THE NEXT THREE DAYS, COLOR IN THE CLOCK DIALS AT THE START OF EACH DAY, APPORTIONING YOUR IDEAL TIME SPENT ON THE VARIOUS ACTIVITIES.

DAY 4

AM ROUTINE

PM ROUTINE

DAY 5

AM ROUTINE

PM ROUTINE

DAY 6

AM ROUTINE

PM ROUTINE

Did you make time for the creative activities you wanted to do? (It's likely that you'll have seen a positive difference when you began the day with an awareness of time, rather than wondering how it ran away from you.)

REPEAT YOUR RITUALS

Decide how you want to prepare to get into the creative zone, then make sure you repeat this ritual every time you begin, so your brain comes to recognize it as a sign that creative work will follow. Rituals can help reduce resistance to creative work, as they set up a rhythm that helps get you into the flow. You don't need to be a genius to be creative. You just need to be consistent in giving yourself time to create.

RITUALS TO TRY

Rearranging your desk (see page 117)

Doodling (see page 78)

Drinking coffee

Lighting a candle

Choosing an affirmation card (see page 48)

Doing a yoga stretch

Listening to music

Taking a short, brisk walk

resisting creativity

So, you've scheduled your creative time. Are you stepping into it effortlessly, or are you resisting? You've planned a walk, a trip, or a session of writing or making something. You're about to begin, feel edgy, and decide to browse the net for a while first–or anything that will delay you getting going. Your resistance will invent a host of merry excuses: Mercury, the planet of communication, is retrograde; maybe you shouldn't begin when it's raining, since that always brings on a low mood; or the contents of the refrigerator are more interesting.

In my experience, when you are in a state of resistance, it's because something is at stake. Creativity involves personal risk–you are allowing part of you, your beliefs and ideas, to take form, and your creative work has the power to change and transform you in a profound way. Resistance likes things to stay as they are. We can see it winning in those who dream and talk about what they want to do, but back off the instant there's a chance to make it happen in the real world. Living with the dream rather than getting down to the work of creating means there's no chance of failure–but there's also no chance of success. Learn to recognize resistance when it's around, and you'll push through it–and continue with what you set out to do.

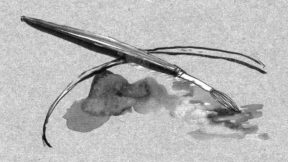

FEELING RESISTANCE

IS A SURE SIGN THAT WHAT YOU WANT TO CREATE IS IMPORTANT

RESISTANCE-BUSTING TIPS

• The aim is to begin. If you can't get going within the first half-hour of creative work, go do something else for an hour, then go back to it. Read, clean, phone, walk … then go back to your creative work. It doesn't matter if you can't keep going for the whole time you've allocated—an hour's productive work is fine.

• Habit helps. The more you keep to your creative timeslot, the easier it becomes.

• Don't judge what you're doing. Reviewing what you did last time gets you into judgment mode, so when you begin, go straight to the next chapter, or the next piece you're making.

• Get into the right-brain mode with the creative crunch exercise on page 109.

• Tackle other challenging situations at the beginning of the day. If you put off that difficult phone call, meeting, or budget, guilt gathers. This feeling sits between you and creativity, like a boulder in the road that you'd rather drive around than shift. Take on what you're resisting straight away. Blow up the boulder, and you're metaphorically free to drive up the creative highway for the rest of the day.

• You don't need to be at a desk or in a studio to be creative. In fact, going somewhere that feels impersonal to you is many an artist's panacea. If you usually sit at a desk, go to a coffee shop (J. K. Rowling began writing the Harry Potter series in the back room of the Elephant House coffee shop in Edinburgh). If you're traveling, don't dismiss your hotel room as a creative space—there's an advantage to having no homely distractions. Maya Angelou chose to write her books in hotel rooms she rented by the month, although she had a house in the same town. She didn't sleep in the hotel, but went there in the mornings purely to write.

DEALING WITH DEADLINES

Realistic deadlines can be brilliant motivators, helping you to plan your time and deliver your work. They also help you to break down a project into bite-size, manageable chunks.

From regular deadlines, good habits form. And deadlines can become easier to meet when we've done it all before, when we know, more or less, what will be involved (although this doesn't discount the effort involved in the creating).

Some deadline pressure can make us thrive, and the adrenaline that is released when we're single-minded and focused on one goal gives us a high; sometimes we're pushed out of our comfort zones and even learn a skill relatively quickly because the deadline exists.

The author Stephen King writes ten pages (about 2,000 words) every day, seven days a week. He has done this for many years, and is an experienced "deadliner"–he knows what works for him. Dickens's first novel, *The Pickwick Papers*, began in 1836 as a series of sketches originally entitled *The Posthumous Papers of the Pickwick Club*, published every month in the *Morning Chronicle* newspaper. Many a contemporary writer has followed the same path: *Bridget Jones's Diary* (1996) by Helen Fielding began life in *The Telegraph*, while Armistead Maupin's acclaimed novel series *Tales of the City* (1978–), on life in San Francisco in the 1970s and 1980s, first appeared in the *San Francisco Chronicle*. No doubt the strict deadlines motivated the authors–as did the promise of regular paychecks.

THE FIVE-MINUTE COUNTDOWN

Here's a fast way to get creative—make yourself write (or be otherwise creative) for a whole five minutes.

- Set your deadline (see suggestions below).

- Five minutes before you have to leave, write or draw for five minutes only. If you're writing, don't let the pen leave the paper. Don't stop until it's time to go, but do leave on time; you have just five minutes. Use the prompt opposite for your first attempt.

- You may well see an idea emerging at the end of the allocated time. Because you have just five minutes, you're not weighed down with self-expectation to produce a brilliant design or write a novel—and you just might spark off an idea that will lead to a project.

SET A DEADLINE

The time you usually leave home in the morning
(for work, school run, gym)

A time you need to leave to get to an appointment
(doctor, optician, interview, meeting)

A time in the evening you need to leave to arrive at an event
(a concert, meeting a friend, a class)

TODAY THE WEATHER IS ...

....

....

....

THE LAST TIME I FELT LIKE THIS WAS:

....

....

....

....

....

....

....

....

....

....

....

....

....

....

....

....

You can also write in the notes program on your phone, or type on your laptop. You might play the piano, start a poem, or sketch a mind map (see page 133).

dissolving blocks to creativity

The phrase "creative block" is negative in itself, conjuring up the idea of an immovable obstruction that will take the equivalent of a psychological bulldozer to break through. But the joy of the block is that it is our own. It is our responsibility, and it is within our power to embrace it, then dissolve it by changing the way we think. A block may come to any creator, and it's an opportunity, every time, to come into a deeper understanding of the self. No ideas? Unable to start or finish a project? Welcome to the creative unblocker.

"BLOCK" ATTITUDES QUIZ

Take a look at the statements opposite and tick the ones that you agree with most strongly, then see the key that follows for the letter (F, R, P, or C) that comes up most often. Try not to think too much about each question, and go with your first response each time.

If you agree with four or more of these statements, it's likely that you are avoiding creative expression. Sometimes we sabotage ourselves rather than deal with the challenges that being creative can bring up.

I don't think I was creative when I was younger and I can't learn it now (F) ☐

I'll be creative when I've got time, maybe when the children have left home, or we've moved house, or when my job isn't so demanding—creative people don't have all the demands I have to deal with (R) ☐

There's no point in trying to make anything because other people do it so much better (C) ☐

I just help people with their problems, I'm not creative as such (F) ☐

I'm not inspired, I mustn't have the gift of creativity (F) ☐

I'm getting too old to do the things I wanted to do (F/R) ☐

I can't finish anything I start (F/P) ☐

I have very high standards for myself (P) ☐

I need money to be creative (R) ☐

Fill in your results:

F: _____   R: _____   P: _____   C: _____

WHAT DO MY RESULTS MEAN?

The biggest blocks to creativity are:

(F) Fear of success, fear of failure, fear of exposure, often expressed as self-judgment

(R) Resentment, in that other people have better circumstances for a creative lifestyle

(P) Perfectionism, often expressed as the inability to finish a project, or the need to delay

(C) Comparison with others

FEAR: DEALING WITH THE SABOTEUR WITHIN

One simple truth is that by trusting ourselves to deal with the risk and reward that creativity offers, we can work through the blocks we put in our way. Being creative can mean taking emotional risks–you are inviting change, which can feel both exciting and uncomfortable. Allow your creative juices to flow and let your dreams take form, and instantly you've created an object, a focus for the attention of other people.

We may fear criticism, but often it's our own self-judgment that's the real problem. Some part of us decides to get in there first, sabotaging our fledgling project with negative thoughts before it's even begun. We wouldn't treat a child that way, so begin to consider your creative output as your baby, which needs protection, not criticism. To overcome fear, you might try:

• Generating a sense of detachment. Observe yourself: while you're creating, imagine a part of you is acting as a witness and appreciating your activity (look, I'm picking up a pen, using some color, stitching, icing, choosing photos … that's interesting, I like that shade …). This gives the non-fearful, creative aspect of yourself a voice.

• Trusting yourself. You are the best person to be working on this project, and good enough to do whatever you like. Try saying some of the affirmations on page 11.

- Working with some of the Play exercises on pages 76–80 as preparation, to free up your ideas.

- Remember that we are all naturally creative, and we are built this way to benefit our well-being. You have an absolute right to create, and to enjoy it.

RESENTMENT: THE MYTH OF THE IVORY TOWER

The perception that creative people live a life detached from society is a romantic ideal that I call the myth of the ivory tower. We might imagine a young, privileged artist in a shabby-chic writing room, about to embark on his next masterpiece. Heeding the call of the Muse, he has all the time in the world to ponder his next verb while his butler tops up his gin and tonic. Or, less imaginatively, you may simply envy someone you know who appears to have more time or money to "indulge" their creative streak.

If this resonates with you, you may be exhibiting an attitude of "poverty consciousness"– when you feel time-poor, or cash-poor, or poor in some other way, and that life isn't fair. This sense of deprivation, no matter how well under control, can produce seeds of negativity that grow in the way of your natural creativity. To combat resentment, you might try:

- Making small changes to your daily routine to make time for creativity; this can have a positive effect on your self-belief (see page 86).

- Being kind to yourself, and seeing the positive aspects of your daily life, by listing your achievements at the end of every day for a week or so, then reflecting on how well you've managed.

- Doing the limitation exercise on page 110 to help you focus.

- Turning negative feelings into creative projects by using any feelings of resentment and anger to tell your life story (see page 17).

PERFECTIONISM AND COMPARISON WITH OTHERS

These two creative mind-blocks are often connected: if we're perfect, we protect ourselves from critical feedback and avoid being seen as inferior to others. Perfectionism can be the block that prevents us from finishing a project, but in fact it often conceals a fear of exposure. If your painting, music, writing, quilting, sculpture, or short film is out there in the world, you'll need to deal with how it's received.

• Writing or illustrating your life story (as on pages 16–23) can help dissolve the blocks of perfectionism and comparison. Creative writing tutor Claire Gillman says: "Telling your story is a safe place to begin creative work, because no one can say what you write isn't true, or criticize it."

• If you think fear is at the heart of your perfectionism, see the tips for combatting fear on the previous pages.

MOVING INTO THE RIGHT-BRAIN ZONE

The right brain can be perceived as visual and intuitive. According to neurosurgeon Richard Bergland, the right brain "thinks in patterns, or pictures," while the left brain can be understood as rational and analytical, processing thoughts as numbers, letters, and words to form logical sequences.

We experience conflict–a creative "crunch"–when we're trying to be creative because our sensible left brains are constantly engaged. This is the part of us that is assessing our creative output as it happens, and unless we can get completely into the right-brain zone, we're constantly switching between left- and right-brain thinking. This switching creates a sense of conflict, doubt, and struggle. The left brain can manifest as the voice that asks how practical your idea is; if it's comparable with others' ideas or output; and if it's good enough.

THE FEELINGS OF CRUNCHING

Mild anxiety

Pressure to perform

Your mind is a blank

Poor concentration

WAYS WE "CRUNCH"

- Writing fiction while constantly revising previous paragraphs lets the left brain in, constantly interrupting the right brain, which just wants to create, unhindered.

- When reading and playing music, we're using the left brain–interpreting symbols, or notes, into meaningful sequences through sound. In improvised music, there are no notes, or very few, and musicians are free to play whatever they like. They must tune in completely to the feel of the sound and the sense of the other musicians, and then play something original. If they have to read music and improvise within the same piece, they have to switch modes instantly. Of course, at a professional level this comes with practice, but learning musicians struggle to shift between reading mode and improvising mode; they cannot instantly make the transition and maintain the same standard of playing in both modes.

- Imagine sitting in a business meeting going through figures. At the end of the meeting, someone asks for ideas for the theme of the summer party. There's often an ominous silence–this is the sound of the left brain struggling to let go so the right brain can engage, and let ideas and inspiration come through.

SHIFT OUT OF YOUR CRUNCH

If you're struggling to access the right-brain state of mind, try the following exercise. You can spend just a minute on it, or turn it into a longer meditation, depending on how you feel and where you are. With practice, you will be able to do it very naturally, and use it whenever you want to shift gear and de-stress.

- Turn your attention from your mind to your body—feel your feet on the floor, the weight of your body in your chair.

- Move a little. Adjust your sitting position, stretch your neck. This helps release mental intensity and reconnects you with your senses and emotions.

- Focus on your breathing—this helps you feel more relaxed and centered. Be aware of your out-breath and try to extend it to a count of five or six, then pause before inhaling. Do this three or four times.

- Conjure up a favorite image: trees swaying in the breeze, you on a sun lounger; recall a favorite song and sense the vibration of the music; or visualize a color that makes you feel good.

- Imagine the right side of your brain filling with light, and a little door to your left brain closing. Stay with this image for a few moments.

THE GIFTS OF LIMITATION

There's a saying that limitation forces invention. Give yourself a zero budget, and see what you can create.

ITEMS YOU MIGHT COLLECT FOR YOUR CREATION

A well-thumbed paperback

Vintage fabric from a friend

Found objects to photograph or video, such as feathers, wood, stones

Used envelopes or shopping receipts

Ring-pulls from cola cans

An item you trade

Technology can also help us create the limitation that forces creativity. Influential British artist David Hockney used the iPad to create 51 drawings, part of his celebrated project *The Arrival of Spring in Woldgate, East Yorkshire in 2011*. You might like to limit yourself to creating something only on your phone–recording sounds, taking pictures, writing only on the Notes app. What possibility does this kind of limitation offer?

WRITE OR DRAW SOMETHING ONLY WITH YOUR NON-DOMINANT HAND.

Try painting with only your feet or hands. No brush allowed!

everyday creativity

Doing a small activity every day can spark your ingenuity and encourage you to trust your creative abilities. It takes the pressure off yourself–you don't have to think of and work on a huge project to be creative.

MAKE SOMETHING YOU'LL NEED FOR YOUR PROJECT

By making something that you will use for your project, you help prepare yourself for creative work without the pressure to begin the project itself. Work around your project to keep the energy flowing.

THINGS YOU COULD MAKE

A journal decorated with your favorite motifs

A quill pen from a feather

A bag for your craft materials

CREATE A NEW EMAIL SIGN-OFF

For your personal email accounts, add something about you after your usual signature at the start of the week. Personal disclosure means a lot to others. They see your values and attitudes and get to know you, which is vital if you're (digitally) marketing yourself and your projects; others need to know that you are open, curious, and authentic. You can also create a new email sign-off to help set your positive intention for the day or week (see page 74). Try out some ideas for your sign-off here.

THIS WEEK, I'M THINKING ABOUT BEGINNING ...

THIS WEEK, I'M SENDING MY SUPPORT TO ...

THIS WEEK, I'M PROUD TO SAY THAT ...

TRY A BINAURAL BEAT

Creativity can be enhanced by sound, according to the developers of binaural beats. Binaural beats are sounds played at different frequencies to induce particular states of consciousness: creativity, meditation, better memory, pain management, relaxation, lucid dreaming, and deep sleep. A binaural soundtrack is best experienced through headphones, as sound of slightly different frequencies goes to each ear, to be processed by the brain as a beating sound. The brain becomes "entrained" to this pulse, matching its frequency.

• Download a binaural app and choose an audio file according to how you'd like to feel, from an "espresso shot" for vitality through a creativity boost–a fascinating way to get into the zone.

• Try listening to a track before you begin a project and/or during work, and see if it helps your ideas flow.

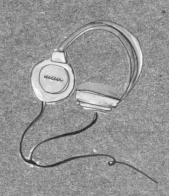

WRITE IT DOWN NOW

Keep a pocket-sized notebook with you wherever you go, or use your phone's voice recorder. When you get an idea, write it down or speak it. We might vow to remember ideas, but in reality, we don't; there's always another distraction or conversation that diverts us almost instantly. Later, when you have time to work on your creative projects, play back or reread your collected notes and recordings. This is valuable material that will spark your imagination, and it's much better than facing a blank page.

WRITE DOWN ANY IDEAS—NOW!

WRITE A SIX-WORD STORY

Ernest Hemingway's famous six-word story, which he apparently wrote for a bet, reads:
"For sale: Baby shoes, never worn." A lesser example is my friend Samantha's attempt:
"Met, fed, bed, slept, left. End?"

WRITE YOUR SIX-WORD STORY.

You might try writing your six-word story in five minutes (see the Five-minute Countdown on page 100), using your own words or the words and phrases list on page 136 for inspiration. Or, set yourself a task to write a six-word story each day for one week.

DESIGN YOUR DESK FOR CREATIVITY

Beginning each day with a small practical task, such as tidying and arranging your workspace, helps you prepare for the mental tasks ahead.

• Prepare the space first: clear away any clutter and clean the desktop.

• In feng shui, the art of placing objects to enhance positive energy (or chi), the desk can be divided into the nine sectors of the Ba Gua, an ancient map that links compass sectors with life areas. The creativity area is traditionally located center right on your desk. You can keep your Creativity Journal here, along with any research notes, materials, collections, and notebooks, and keep it free from objects associated with problems (complaints, clutter, bills).

• The creativity area is also linked with the element of metal, so metal items (paperweights or silver picture frames, for example) are believed to raise the chi energy here, giving your creative projects a boost.

THERE ARE LIMITLESS
CREATIVE WAYS
TO THINK
OUTSIDE THE BOX

grow your ideas

how do we create?

The French polymath and philosopher Henri Poincaré (1854–1912) believed that the process of creating happens in four phases.

1. PREPARATION

The ideas phase, when you might brainstorm or research your creative project, or set about solving a problem using tried-and-tested techniques.

2. INCUBATION

The phase in which ideas are combined in the unconscious mind when we're doing something else. (Without the unconscious stage–the time to process our ideas internally–it's less likely that we'll be able to create, or complete our creation.)

3. ILLUMINATION (THE "FLASH")

According to Poincaré, this is dependent on the groundwork we've already done: "Sudden illumination [is] a manifest sign of long, unconscious prior work."

4. EVALUATION

Appraising your work.

FINDING INSPIRATION

The following activities will lead you through Poincaré's four stages of creativity.

PREPARATION

WRITE DOWN FIVE THINGS THAT CAPTIVATE OR INSPIRE YOU.

1 ....

2 ....

3 ....

4 ....

5 ....

- Now make a connection. By this, I mean work out why that particular thing inspires you. What is it about falling leaves, or about a red moon?

- Go deeper with this connection. You might also find yourself connecting two or more things that come up on your list. Write them down. You might want to look at the phrases on page 136 and choose two at random, and see how they might connect ("cross words" and "peace"; "music helps" and "finding answers.") Jot down whatever springs to mind.

- If you need to, do some research—search your memory or the internet, and talk to people who can contribute to your idea or knowledge.

- Think of this phase as like baking a cake without a recipe. You need the ingredients (ideas), then you must mix them up so they connect with one another.

WHAT MEANINGS/CONNECTIONS CAN YOU SEE IN YOUR FIVE
INSPIRING THINGS?

....
....
....
....
....
....
....
....
....
....

INCUBATION

Let your ideas sit for a while—come back to this page in a few days or weeks. As the cake
needs to bake, so your ideas are taking form without your conscious involvement. The
important thing is to trust the process.

ILLUMINATION AND EVALUATION

This is the "Eureka!" moment, the point at which the problem is solved, or the idea, or cake, comes together; you suddenly know that what you've made will hold, and/or get a sense of what else you might need to do to make progress. The ingredients have come together to create something original. The cake's coming out of the oven and, as you greet it, be open to what it might look like. It could be different from what you first imagined. (If the cake isn't ready, let it bake a little longer.)

Do you like the cake? Does it look and taste good to your eye and palate? Be generous in your appreciation. Accept what you've made, however it turned out.

DESCRIBE YOUR IDEA, AND HOW YOU FEEL ABOUT IT.

a thought walk

Taking a "thought walk," a phrase coined by the eighteenth-century philosopher Jean-Jacques Rousseau, is a time-honored tradition among creative people, helping them to think, plot, dream, and problem-solve; Charles Dickens walked to ruminate, as did Mark Twain and Sigmund Freud.

Moving our bodies through walking seems to move stuck dialogue, while the new places we see on our walks offer new perspective on old problems. If you're having a creative block or trying to solve a problem, try this.

• Set an intention to take your idea or problem with you and give it some air. Go for a walk at your usual pace, then begin to slow down. Run through all the possible scenarios attached to your problem as if you're running a mini-movie in your mind. Now visualize that the movie is still running, but at the back of your mind, rather than in front of you. Begin to observe what's going on around you.

• What you notice on your walk can be metaphors for new approaches and solutions. For example, roadworks might suggest that you need to cordon off the part of the problem that causes most disruption, and ask experts (like the maintenance crew you see) for support. You might link the pigeons fighting over breadcrumbs with you and the management structure in your company, or gain perspective on your dilemma when you see a child enjoying an ice cream. Make the connections between the problem and the external world. What you notice can unlock solutions and inspire you to think differently.

WRITE DOWN WHAT YOU NOTICED ON YOUR WALK. CAN YOU SEE ANY CONNECTIONS BETWEEN THAT AND WHAT'S BEEN ON YOUR MIND?

"I can only meditate when I am walking. When I stop, I cease to think; my mind only works with my legs."

Jean-Jacques Rousseau

begin with the brainstorm

Brainstorming suggests creative chaos, a storm within the mind. Ideas are blown about, with new concepts spiraling in the sky, tornado-style. In business, the brainstorm often requires participants to sit round a boardroom table and throw phrases up into the air or at one another.

Brainstorming, however, also works for individuals, and is perhaps even more effective if you're doing it alone with just your paper and pen (brainstorming in a group may actually be limited by social inhibition).

WHAT DOES BRAINSTORMING INVOLVE?

Gathering ideas, and drawing them or writing them down as you go

Including all the possibilities, no matter how random

Using free association

Letting ideas flow without self-judgment

Making new connections between ideas

YOUR LONE BRAINSTORM

On the following page, you can create a brainstorm around an idea or problem.

• First, get some positive energy flowing for a few minutes—sketch, play your favorite music, or think of a mentor or celebrity you admire: generate a happy feeling.

• Set a time limit. This is the length of time you will put ideas to paper. After your allocated time is up, your unconscious mind will continue to process and formulate ideas when you start doing something else—washing dishes, walking to work, having a meeting on an unrelated topic, so there's no pressure to generate solutions immediately.

• Write down your goal or dilemma in the center of the paper.

• In pictures and/or words, put down whatever comes into your mind around the goal/dilemma. Move fast and keep going. Don't assess your work at this stage.

• When you've finished, take a break. Do something else.

• Later, review your work—what ideas do you respond to the most? Which ones give you a buzz? Some might surprise you.

• Give your brainstorming work a title and a date.

Imagine that your pen is connected to your mind. Your hand is just a tool to get the ideas down.

BRAINSTORM WITH FREE WRITING

Free writing is a great way to work through procrastination and other blocks, and it's a technique used by many creative-writing teachers to get students into the flow of ideas without stopping to self-assess.

The next two pages of this journal are for your free-writing brainstorm.

• Write quickly, and don't pay attention to spelling or grammar. This can feel quite exposing at first, as if you're writing like a child, focusing only on the idea or the story. But writing without worrying about punctuation and correct spelling keeps your right brain engaged, without allowing the left brain to jump in and assess what you're doing— which can hinder the creative flow.

• Fill both pages, and don't read what you've written until you've finished. You might find yourself wanting to write out clutter first, beginning with to-do lists or shopping lists, to get immediate worries out of the way so that unconscious creative ideas can come through.

TODAY I'M FEELING AS THOUGH I MIGHT...

mind-mapping

The mind map is a focused method of looking at ways to work toward goals and solutions. It takes the form of an image that reflects your thoughts, associations, and ideas, and shows how they might connect, helping you see paths to your goals and break through problems. Mind maps are the brainchild of neuro-linguistic programming pioneer Tony Buzan, and can help you see new, creative ways to approach any situation.

THE WORDLESS MIND MAP

By working with pictures rather than words, you connect with the creative right brain. When you assess what you've drawn, you're using your logical left brain, judging the content and editing down the tasks. Follow your mind map, and you'll be able to work more effectively to unravel a problem, or to shape your project or idea. You can create a mind map on the opposite page.

• Begin by drawing your main goal in the center of the page. Now draw branches coming off it, placing other ideas on the branches, then adding sub-branches for less important ideas or associations. Link any connected task with a line.

• When you've finished, look again at the goal you've drawn in the center. Now assess all the branches, and cross out those that don't directly support your goal. This should leave you with only the actions and ideas that will create the outcome you want.

DRAW YOUR WORDLESS MIND MAP.

oblique strategies

Brian Eno and his friend the painter Peter Schmidt created 100 Oblique Strategy cards, each with a printed message, to inspire lateral thinking. Lateral thinking, first described in 1967 by the doctor and author Edward de Bono, is an approach that uses creative, indirect ways to stimulate solutions, rather than using imagination or step-by-step logic.

Chosen at random, the cards' messages are not considered final solutions or direct instructions, but rather prompts to find alternative ways of thinking–particularly when you're working under pressure. Each card has a statement or a question, such as:

- "Tidy up"

- "Destroy: Nothing."

- "Destroy: The most important thing."

- "Who should be doing this job?"

- "How would they do it?"

"The function of the Oblique Strategies was, initially, to serve as a series of prompts which said, 'Don't forget that you could adopt this attitude,' or 'Don't forget you could adopt that attitude'."

Brian Eno

MAKE YOUR OWN CARDS

There are 100 cards in the Oblique Strategies deck, but you can make your own with fewer messages. The trick is to make the subjects of the messages as diverse as you can, by choosing them randomly from a range of sources. For example:

• Take a favorite novel or a dictionary. Flick through the pages, stop at random, and choose statements, speech, or one word and write it down. (You could also do this with a self-help book, a cookbook, poetry, or a newspaper or magazine.)

• The internet: use the word "proverb" or "quotation" as a search term, and click on one of the results at random. Or pick a news story and choose the tenth and fifteenth words or phrases from the first sentence or paragraph. If you have a lucky number, use this to pick your messages. Keep it random.

• Use nuggets of overheard conversation as source material.

• Use the word and phrase lists overleaf.

Write each message on a blank card, about the size of a business card, leaving the reverse of the card blank. Keep the cards in your desk drawer or purse, and when you need to make a decision or solve a difficult problem, take five minutes with your cards and draw one or more at random, face down. Then see how your card message(s) offer an alternative approach.

WORDS AND PHRASES

Your intuition is telling you	Still waters
Less is more	It's in the detail
Slow it down	Once upon a time ...
Cross words	Walk
It doesn't always rain	Amazing grace
Take time out	You know best
Peace	What if this is the last time?
Too clever?	My ideas are infinite
Music helps	See the beauty
Be still	Finding answers
Use a picture instead	Stone circle
See it in black and white	Be the teacher
What's missing?	Indulge
Look to the stars	Blue
Keep trying	

LIST YOUR OBLIQUE STRATEGY CARDS HERE.

- ....
- ....
- ....
- ....
- ....
- ....
- ....
- ....
- ....
- ....
- ....
- ....
- ....
- ....

NOW MAKE YOUR CARDS!

feeding the flow

Many successful businesses are based on partnership. From Barnes & Noble, Rolls-Royce, and Laurel and Hardy to Lennon and McCartney and Dolce & Gabbana, they all began with two people having a conversation, and deciding to work together rather than alone.

When we collaborate, it helps us make new connections, push boundaries, and reach beyond our individual interests. Creative pairs often complement each other, pooling their own unique skills and perspectives, and so a creative partnership can be greater than the sum of its parts.

COLLABORATION
FEEDS
CREATIVITY

THE CREATIVE HOOK-UP

Partner with a friend, acquaintance, or social-media contact who works in a different discipline—for example, if you bake, hook up with a writer; if you like fashion, pair up with a poet. Come up with an idea together in a week, beginning with a conversation over coffee or a glass of wine. What would you like to make together? Share your interests. Your collaboration is about making connections, sensing how one discipline can feed another. Cake story? A poem inspired by Coco Chanel's sunglasses?

NAME THREE PEOPLE YOU COULD COLLABORATE WITH.

1 ....

2 ....

3 ....

NOW GET IN TOUCH WITH THEM!

THE SOCIAL MEDIA REVOLUTION

Social media makes it possible to go beyond the traditional pairings and communicate with networks of fellow creatives for feedback, support, and stimulation. You can brainstorm ideas with kindred spirits on innovation sites such as IdeaScale. Alternatively, investigate crowdfunding for your project by using a crowdfunding website to attract backing from the public, who get to be involved with the project as it progresses. Crowdfunding has been used to attract individual contributions toward scientific research, environmental initiatives, movie-making, video games, music, and products from customized watches to skateparks or graphic novels. It supports both new ventures and established artists who want to avoid traditional routes to market.

In 2005, American composer Maria Schneider won a Grammy music award for her ArtistShare release *Concert in the Garden*. And in 2012, Musician Amanda Palmer, formerly of the Dresden Dolls, raised over $1 million through Kickstarter to fund her album *Theatre is Evil*.

Many authors and artists now use the direct connection they have with their readers through social media. It provides a way to invite their fans to be part of their projects and to develop a broad, loyal fan base, without investing money.

You, too, can put your ideas out on social media: look for groups that share your interests, and ask for creative companions to brainstorm with.

English author Silvia Hartmann wrote her fantasy novel *The Dragon Lords* (2012) live in Google Docs, so fans could see her writing in real time and give feedback about the plot and characters as the story progressed. And in 2014 the award-winning English novelist David Mitchell, author of *Cloud Atlas* (2004) and *Ghostwritten* (1999), took to Twitter to share his new short story, *The Right Sort*, in 367 tweets.

WAYS TO CONNECT

Social media: Facebook, Instagram, Twitter

Publish your work: Tumblr, Medium, Wordpress

Crowdfund: Crowdfunder, ArtistShare, Kickstarter, Patreon

commit to your creativity

When you do what you love, it's much easier to commit to it. Without commitment, we never really know if we can succeed. Creative commitment is both attitude and action; when you're not actively working on a project, keep hold of your creative awareness. Take it with you wherever you go, letting it guide you toward opportunities to write, paint, discuss, share, and be inspired.

Commitment looks different to different people: for some of you, it might mean committing time, regularly, to your creative project (see page 86 for ideas); for others, talking about your projects with others is a big commitment step.

I spent years telling people I'd just met that the books I commissioned were on "mind, body, spirit" subjects, then qualified it by saying "yoga, complementary therapies …" –at which they'd nod and agree. The truth was that these were the areas of my work I was least interested in, but I thought they sounded more palatable than the truth, which was that I wrote and commissioned books on spiritual subjects.

These days I tell everyone exactly what I do, and if they don't like it, fine–but I generally find that most people respond positively, maybe because they can see that I'm passionate about and committed to my work, and that I don't avoid sharing that.

When you feel you're committing time, truth, and energy to your creative projects, it's worth evaluating this commitment as you go along, at each stage of your project.

WRITE DOWN HOW YOU'RE GOING TO COMMIT
TO YOUR CREATIVITY FROM NOW ON.

"Creativity arises from a constant churn of ideas, and
one of the easiest ways to encourage that fertile froth
is to keep your mind engaged with your project. When you
work regularly, inspiration strikes regularly."

Gretchen Rubin, author of The Happiness Project (2010)